Why Am I So Angry and Stressed All the Time?

The Hidden Secret of Anger and Stress in Our Lives

Diana Loera

Table of Contents

Introduction

Ever wake up angry?

Do you wonder why people look and act so happy and meanwhile you'd like pummel your pillow (and maybe you have already done so)?

In this day and age, most of us are constantly on the go and/or worried –

How will we pay an upcoming bill?

What if I'm laid off work?

If the escrow amount rises one more time on my house payment.... (and of course, it does).

Why can't my kids be on time?

Why can't anyone pick up this house?

Why does my co-worker think it is okay to dump work on me?

Why did my spouse cheat on me?

Why do my siblings think I should shoulder the burden of caring for our elderly parents?

The list is endless and there is no reprieve.

Meanwhile, we get up and carry this anger and stress around all day. It sometimes keeps us up at night too.

Where did this come from? Will it ever end? How does one handle it?

These feelings are far more common than you may realize. You are not alone. You are not a bad person because you feel angry and stressed.

Now more than ever, people are struggling with feelings of stress and anger.

But what most people don't know is that there are many hidden red flags before we reach the boiling over point.

In this book we'll be going through the feelings of anger and stress as well as red flags that help us recognize impending problems.

Our end goal is improving your life, recognizing what triggers these feelings – and cutting them off at the pass.

At the end of this book, you'll find a workbook has been included. As you progress through this book you'll also find some questions and space to write your answers.

This isn't a quiz – this is your own unique workbook and there are no right or wrong answers.

You can work on it at your own pace and ideally, using the workbook will help you shed light on why you react as you do and things you can do to alleviate stress and feelings of anger.

The Root of the Problem

As we take a closer look at what is causing your stress and anger, we'll need to drill down to the root of the matter.

One feeling we'll be covering is resentment. Resentment is not a pretty word. When we think of someone being resentful, we may think of someone who is jealous or pouting.

In actuality, resentment is the warning flag before anger. Resentment isn't the full blown pissed off, stressed and angry mode – it is the danger, danger warning to protect us from anger – if we recognize it quick enough.

Resentment is when you realize in the back of your mind you are being treated unfairly. You may also be triggering a similar situation that adds fuel to the fire of a current one.

When not resolved, the resentment moves into anger and of course, stress.

You may be resentful when you are disappointed because (once again) someone didn't do something that was promised – such as taking out the trash on garbage day. Leaving you, once again, to have to do it as, garbage pick- up is once a week and you don't want cans of garbage sitting for yet another week.

For some, the garbage example may sound trivial. However, we each have our own resentments and what is trivial for one person, may be a huge issue for someone else.

Don't compare yourself to others. If something gives you a feeling of resentment, anger or stress – so be it.

We want to find what triggers these feelings in you so you can handle and eliminate them.

You deserve to be happy, stress free and relaxed so let's start looking at the process your mind goes through that causes feelings of anger and stress.

The Face of Resentment

Anger and resentment might be natural emotions that we experience but holding onto those feelings can only have a negative effect on your life. You need to explore your feelings, get to know your triggers and work through the resentment you have been dealing with.

What does resentment look like?

It's when you harbor animosity, have unresolved anger, you have an aching, seething turmoil within you when an issue is discussed, a lack of forgiveness, distrust, or unresolved grief.

It can manifest in a manner of ways from silent fuming to angry internal dialogues towards that person but within yourself, engaging in obsessive and ruminating thinking about the person and/or event to having nightmares.

Resentment can develop when you don't assert your feelings when someone mistreats you.

You may start to feel resentful after someone takes advantage of you, when others succeed without working as hard as you, when put in an impossible situation, when embarrassed, rejected consistently, ignored, put down, or victimized.

When resentment goes unresolved you may feel touchy or on edge, you may feel hostile, sarcastic, and cynical.

You may struggle to build healthy relationships because of your general distrust and inability to open up to others.

With resentment comes irrational thinking that undermines your happiness and well-being.

All in all, you are not your usual self and are unhappy more and more.

Minor and Major Resentments

When it comes to that feeling of resentment, we tend to find two types –minor ones which are short term and major ones which are long term.

A minor resentment is one that is usually something you are irked about, but it blows over fairly quick and is done.

A major resentment hangs around long afterwards and steadily builds – this is the danger red flag one, more so than the minor resentment.

As mentioned earlier, anger is the most common and generally the most significant emotion linked to resentment.

Anger can cause one to impulsively say something without thinking. We've all done it – blurted something when upset. The lack of control of our emotions can be at a higher level when we are angry.

If one reaches that major resentment level, they roll over the dam, just like Niagara Falls, to anger.

Anger not checked, can go into rage. Harboring resentments holds you back in multiple ways – it can escalate to anger and even rage. It can also cause you to stress, worry and replay situations over and over in your head.

Typically, more time is spent replaying an event the larger the problem was for you or if it tends happen over and over. Keep in mind, there are times when resentment (and anger) is more than justified.

So, with this being said, the truth is that the person holding onto the resentment tends to be the one who suffers the most, while the person who made the problem is many times unaware or simply doesn't care that he or she is causing this problem.

When something happens due to someone close to you versus a stranger, the levels of resentment will be different such as if you caught your spouse in a bold face lie versus the kid at the deli claiming no coleslaw was left when you needed 3 lbs. of it for an office party and you feel the kid was too lazy to go look in the back.

However, in some cases resentment occurs when something doesn't go your way. Such as no coleslaw above.

You expected the kid to behave one way (go look in back) and he instead told you none was available. In due fairness, the kid may have just been back here and indeed none was left but, you were miffed.

This is simply human nature; we are all far from perfect. We need to learn not to allow our feelings to be manipulated and dependent upon how others acted or behaved.

Resentment Red Flags

So how does one decide what could be triggers for resentment?

Some flags are not easy to spot, they tend to just creep up on you. There are some indicators that may help you see a resentment before it escalates to anger.

Do you have a persistent, nagging not so good feeling when a certain person, experience or situation comes to mind?

Do you replay, over and over, something that made you angry and/or stressed?

Do you find yourself gritting your teeth and constantly irritated by one person?

Do you imagine doing some kind of "payback" to a certain person and not a nice payback either.

Do you find yourself feeling small, or not as good as others, especially after interaction with one specific person?

Do you go out of your way to avoid a specific person?

You are not alone. Most people experience at least one of these feelings now and then.

The point now is you are at a fork in the road. One way goes down Resentment Road and the other goes to Peace of Mind Avenue.

The Road to Resentment

Getting to resentment is probably not something you ever imagined would happen.

Resentful feelings are unique, and in most cases, very specific for the person experiencing the feeling.

There are some though which are common hotbeds for resentment.

Health Matters – No matter how much you may love or care for someone, you may feel some resentment at times. Helping someone who is elderly, ill or disabled, tends to have a greater responsibility level.

Discrimination – Racism, Sexism, Discrimination of any kind – is not only wrong but it devalues and degrades people. It can cause feelings of resentment. Even if you are not the target, if you see it happening to family, friends, co-workers and others, it may have an effect on you.

Not a 50/50 Partnership - When one feels like they are constantly pulling the load at home or work, taking on more responsibilities with no appreciation or help day after day, it can cause resentment.

Toxic People - When one is constantly at the effect of a toxic person be it in a work or personal setting and is constantly degraded, insulted, embarrassed or any other trait a toxic person takes joy in spreading, it hurts. Words can and do hurt us and resentful feelings may begin occurring.

Impact of Resentment on You

Fact is, unfortunately, resentment, anger and stress can and will take a toll on you.

In many circumstances, the person causing you to be upset is clueless or occasionally is one who is taking delight in goading you – that's a whole different situation and we will be discussing that type very soon.

For now, let's look at what this unhandled resentment and anger can do to you mentally and physically.

When one harbors anger, resentment and/or stress, you may find yourself with a weakened immune system, stomach issues, a weird mix of aches and pains that never seem to fully go away. Headaches, hormonal issues (such as missed periods), anxiety attacks and even heart problems.

The list continues as one's attitude may go from happy to miserable. One may shout at the kids, be short tempered, lose sleep and simply just not feel happy or relaxed.

Gained some weight? Resentment, anger and stress produces stress related hormones – Cortisol causing you to add weight and struggle to lose it.

Cortisol production is another red flag – our body is truly amazing. It gives us red flags to watch for and Cortisol is the body's main stress hormone. It works with parts of the body to help control things like fear and stress.

Once the fear or stress has passed, Cortisol settles down and life continues. But when stress doesn't go down and is always simmering – Cortisol reacts and can throw the body off track leading to weight gain, headaches, anxiety and more. That belly fat you just can't lose? Cortisol may be the culprit.

Impact of Your Resentment on Others

Sometimes we don't realize, at all, the impact of our resentment on others.

It may be our family, friends, co-workers or random people we pass by.

If you are feeling resentment, you may look like a walking thundercloud and not even realize it.

Catch your reflection randomly in a store window and it may jar you. This is the face others are seeing.

You may be unintentionally short tempered with others, hurting your relationship with them unintentionally. You may be passed over for a promotion at work as it is evident you are not leaving your problems at the door.

This is absolutely not your intention at all but is the effect that resentment, especially unhandled resentment may have on you and those around you.

Recognizing, handling and stopping resentment is crucial for your own well being and also for the wellbeing of others.

Stopping Resentment Before Anger Appears

At this point in the book, you should have a good beginning grasp of what may have pushed you past resentment or you've realized you're in the resentment phase and don't want to slide into anger.

You will need to dig down and make a real effort to intentionally free yourself from the quicksand of resentment before it drags you down further.

If you are well past that phase and are sick and tired of being so angry in what seems like all the time, you may have a bit more work to do to back yourself out of these feelings -but it can be done.

The main thing is recognizing what has gone on to bring you to this point in your life.

Think about and name the situation or it may have been a series of events or actions.

_____

_____

Has this happened to you before with the same person or a different person?

_____

_____

How did you handle the situation at that time?

_____

_____

Resetting Yourself

Just because you've gone through a tough situation, does not mean you will forever be angered and stressed over a situation.

There are some steps to follow that will help you reset and remove stress and anger.

Take a good look at the emotion before resentment – As we've covered, resentment comes before anger.

But before you reached resentment – what triggered it? Was it disappointment or embarrassment or fear? If not one of these, that's okay. What emotion came to mind as you reflected back?

_____

_____

Often feelings such as the above, are the ones right before the feeling of resentment and then anger.

Your next step is to really look closely at that moment and how it made you feel.

In looking back, was your feeling justified?

_____

_____

If when looking back now, do you feel perhaps you did overreact a bit, ideally the feeling of resentment you held will now dwindle down.

_____

_____

But what if your feelings were fully justified? Explain why you think this may be the case.

_____

_____

Take a moment and separate the person involved from the situation. Was it the person or situation? Explain why.

_____

_____

Good people can do and say things, unintentionally, that upset us. Sometimes we harbor resentment towards an individual when our real issue isn't the person but rather their actions or the emotions that were stirred as a result of their actions.

We want to scream when we see, once again, the dishwasher wasn't unloaded and now the sink is overflowing with dishes.

Or employees at the office have, once again, clogged up the drain in the breakroom sink.

Sometimes it seems like a never-ending loop of the same stuff making us short tempered and stressed. It may help you to remember, family, friends, coworkers and the random person on the street are human. We all make non optimum choices and decisions at some time or other in our lives.

Being able to separate the person from their actions and behavior, makes it much easier to not fall in the resentment trap.

When You Simply Cannot Forgive

Sometimes you may feel that you absolutely cannot forgive someone.

It may be that once you've had some time you will eventually forgive the person, or it may be something so grievous that forgiveness may never arrive.

In situations such as these, you need to look at the cause of your resentment and ideally inch your way to some type of forgiveness.

This may cause you to end a relationship and/or friendship, move from where you live or find a new job. If you feel seeing the person involved is causing you great stress over and over, it may call for a disconnecting and relocation.

However, you still will need to handle those feelings. This may take a focused effort and time which is natural. Otherwise, your mind will play the situation over and over which doesn't help you at all.

Your goal at this point isn't a complete erasure of the matter but simply recognizing you are the one suffering from harboring these feelings and the other person most likely doesn't even think about the event.

Forgiveness, once you reach it, will be like a breath of fresh air.

Instead of having the past hanging over you like a black cloud, dragging you down, you can focus on joy in your world and look at the opportunities ahead.

My grandma said to me once that some people are simply steppingstones in someone's life. The bad that they brought with them is only temporary and allows you to step forward - to much better things.

If you can adopt a thought process such as the one above, it may help you find your way to the point of forgiveness.

Creating a Path Towards Forgiveness

I know in some cases; you just don't want to do it. Why should you forgive someone for doing something so stupid, so harmful, so hateful?

You don't need to call the person and proclaim forgiveness. You don't even need to see the person again.

You do need to get the negative feelings out of you.

The goal is not so much a resolution of the issue. The odds are in many cases, most likely the person would never apologize anyways.

This isn't about him or her -it is about you and ridding yourself of that emotional baggage.

Write the person a letter outlining how this has affected you and how you are now firmly closing the door on the matter. You are forgiving them for your own good and moving on. You may find once you do this a huge weigh lifts off of you. Shred the letter when done and consider this as closure as you do so. Dispose of the shredded letter and move on.

Other suggestions are journaling the matter out or talking through the matter with a close friend, family member or counselor.

You will know which suggestion fits you best and the sense of relief once done, will validate success.

Your goal is not the issue of what caused you the pain or stress but releasing the resentment.

This allows you to air the matter and move it out of your head. Otherwise, it will play over and over in your head which does nothing but build up in your mind and hold you back.

What Forgiveness Isn't

As mentioned, forgiveness can make you feel like a huge weight has been removed, the black cloud over your head is gone and you feel lighter.

Forgiveness also may have some additional benefits. You may now feel motivated to exercise more or begin walking daily after work. You may begin eating differently. You may see your clothes fit better as you've lost some weight or became more toned. People may ask your secret, saying you look younger and happier.

Forgiveness isn't easy in many cases. Sometimes it is a long hard road.

Sometimes, a person holds back from practicing forgiveness as they feel if they forgive someone, they are condoning what the person did or said or downplaying how awful it was for them.

Once you flip that forgiveness switch, you will be amazed when you find you feel like a weight came off of you.

Flipping the forgiveness switch often isn't easy but the end result can be very freeing.

Don't feel that practicing forgiveness means you are okay with what was done by that person. That is not the case - at all.

Practicing forgiveness is all about you. Putting you first.

Forgiveness will benefit you in many ways. It lifts that heavy weight off of you. You may have more focus, sleep better and have a much more positive outlook.

After you've forgiven them if you do decide to interact with the person who caused you this anguish and resentfulness, you can immediately negate any hold they had on you before by doing one simple thing.

Making an intentional effort to be kind and compassionate towards them. This does not mean being flowery and gushing. It means taking the high road and showing you have done so by your actions. You don't have to speak with them. You don't have to look at them. Just being around them with a non-hostile attitude and no harsh words. It also leaves the other party with no recourse.

You may find once you have forgiven the person, it is like a deflated balloon. You no longer have any attention on them or what they did to you.

Quick Ways to Move Forward and Keep Resentment Away

Once you've pulled the huge weigh of a resentment off of your shoulders, you'll most likely feel much lighter, more focused and relaxed than you were during the difficult phase.

As you move forward, some steps may be helpful in keeping further resentments at bay.

Adding Relaxation Techniques -

Doing yoga, deep breathing exercises, praying, gratitude, adding a set time for quiet time or meditation – each of these may be helpful to you. Choose one and make a set time daily to do it. Habits are formed in 21 days so work towards 21 consistent days and make a relaxation technique a habit.

Remember to stay in the present. Digging into the past, opens the door to resentment. Keep it closed.

Become a Boundary Setter -

It is sometimes hard to say no. But once you begin setting boundaries, you'll find it may keep further resentments away. Keep your communication clear. Setting a boundary doesn't mean you are being mean to someone. It means you are making time for yourself and not getting roped into things that later may cause resentment.

Be Realistic -

If you are debating on accepting an invite and know most of the guests are heavy smokers and you don't smoke, keep in mind what you will be walking in to. Having a realistic idea about a person or situation beforehand helps you avoid resentment during and after.

Control is out of our hands – maddening as it may be, heavy traffic, long lines, whatever the case, there are things we cannot control. We can't to control others and how they feel and respond too. Keep your expectations real and keep the rose-colored glasses off.

Perfect isn't necessary in many cases. Sure, it sleeted, there was traffic and one of your kids cried, it seemed, incessantly. By no means did this mean the visit to see Santa was a failure. Having a realistic expectation keeps it all in check.

Keep your focus on pursuing what makes you happy. If you've always wanted to do watercolor paintings, sign up for a course. No courses available? Look online. Buy some basic supplies and began teaching yourself. Find the things you want to do and begin, no matter how small your first step may be. Shifting focus keeps negative feelings at bay.

Own Your Resentment

Yes, own it. Claim it. You have resentment. We all do. And today you are doing something about it.

Let's look at some easy ways to own up to resentment and deflate it beginning right now.

1. Accept you have resentment and name what the resentment is over.

_____

_____

2. Accept that this is something that happened in the past and name the time this occurred.

_____

_____

3. Accept that this is YOUR resentment.

_____

_____

4. Decide you are going to handle this resentment – beginning right now.

_____

_____

5. Decide you are going to choose to be happy and move past this resentment – beginning right now.

_____

_____

_____

6. Identify one thing (no matter how small it may seem) that dumping this resentment will make time for.

_____

_____

7. Decide you are going to forgive, forget, whatever you choose – the resentment is now in the past and you are moving forward.

_____

_____

8. Think of yourself waving to that resentment in your rear-view mirror. What do you see? How do you feel?

_____

_____

_____

_____

_____

_____

9. Remember – there is no power in resentment.

_____

_____

10. Remember – you are in control of your life.

_____

_____

Are You Addicted to Stress?

You may have re-read the name of this chapter.

When we think about addictions – we tend to think drugs, gambling, alcohol, smoking and on a lower note, coffee, texting, social media – but being addicted to being stressed?

Stress can be addicting, and one doesn't even realize it is happening.

When we are stressed, one gets that boost of adrenaline and that boost may help focus and power through doing things, at a much quicker pace than usual.

Unfortunately, that boost also floods your body with cortisol which is a hormone.

As the high levels of cortisol flood through your bloodstream, the cortisol hormone increases your appetite, causes insulin resistance and slows your metabolism. This leads the body to store fat and calories to help you cope with stress.

Perhaps you smoke. You may not eat when you are suddenly ravenous, but you may see an increase in smoking.

Cortisol's favorite place for fat is belly fat. That jiggly fat that just doesn't want to go away. Realize you now have a muffin top" – fat overhanging your waistband? That is the effect of cortisol.

When you constantly re-think and tell people about what has made you so resentful you are flooding your body with adrenaline as you relive the issue once again.

Your body likes this rush of adrenaline and you, unknowingly, may be feeding that rush over and over.

Where the problem comes in is unfortunately, it may push people away from you. People may become tired of hearing on an ongoing basis about your resentment.

In the long run, you are not doing yourself any favors by harboring resentment. You are taking up your time and focus, may see a gain in belly fat and you may be pushing people away from you unintentionally.

The Consequences of Not Breaking a Stress Addiction

You know how life goes. There's always something that interrupts your plans, and it happens on the day when you can least afford to encounter something adding stress to your day. You might be on your way to work because you have to go over a project with your boss before the client gets there for a scheduled appointment.

But the next thing you know, you're trapped in a traffic jam. There's no way around it and you can't turn back. You're just stuck. When this happens, your body reacts and floods your system with stress hormones.

The reaction from your body is based on the fight or flight response and it's meant to be a help to you. However, when the situation isn't life or death, this response isn't needed.

When this is an occasional circumstance where you get a flood or stress hormones, it's not a big deal.

But you start to have it even when you're dealing with a mundane stressor because you don't know the right coping techniques to turn to. When your body is constantly getting this flood of hormones, it affects you by giving you that brain chemical high.

It's easy to get addicted to wanting to get that boost of chemicals. You feel good to some degree when you first get it, but over time, this constant cycle of having a stress response within the body wreaks havoc on your physical health.

Over time, the overuse of your stress hormone starts to take a toll on your immune system. This happens because your body has something known as natural killer cells. These are designed to battle against serious conditions such as cancer, but these cells are also designed to fight things like bacterial or viral illnesses.

They work to protect your immunity. Stress weakens the ability of these cells to work the way that they're supposed to, leaving you with little protection so you're constantly catching whatever is going around.

It's not just illnesses that you'll face more often when you fail to break your stress addiction. You'll be at a higher risk for developing conditions that are related to stress such as diabetes.

When you get stressed, it raises your glucose level - even if you don't have the disease.

Stress can make you more likely to have a heart attack because when you're stressed, your blood pressure goes up.

The flood of stress hormones that you get are supposed to temporarily narrow your blood vessels. But when you're addicted to stress, these blood vessels can be constantly narrowed, which restricts blood flow and oxygen to the heart.

When you're stressed, it can also affect your digestive health. You can develop nausea, stomach cramps and suffer from diarrhea or constipation. You can also suffer from heartburn.

People who are addicted to stress can develop reproductive problems. Women might skip a monthly menstrual cycle, or they might notice that their periods last longer, while men can experience lower levels of testosterone, which is linked with impotence.

But it's not just your physical health that will show the signs of stress. You can also struggle with mental health. For many people, prolonged exposure to stress, such as with a stress addiction, can cause depression.

This happens because the stress hormones linger, and you don't get that break from them that you're normally supposed to get. It's common for stress to have an impact on your emotions and when you constantly get that flood of stress hormones, it brings out negative feelings such as grief, which can lead to depression.

Anxiety is another consequence of not dealing with a stress addiction. You don't have to have an anxiety disorder to develop anxiety. This is something that happens as a result of whatever stress you have in your life.

When you have anxiety, it can show up as both physical and emotional symptoms. When it has to do with your mental health, the anxiety that you experience usually reveals itself through a feeling of dread.

You might feel nervous at random times or consistently. Sometimes anxiety can show up as feeling like something is just off. You feel wary. This mental reaction can happen whenever you're about to face a situation or when you think about that situation.

It can also happen because you fear the results of a situation. When stress is what's behind your anxiety, then what you're experiencing lingers and doesn't just go away. Not dealing with stress can also lead to panic attacks.

A panic attack is what happens when you get a feeling of overwhelming fear or you experience a deep anxiety. Panic attacks can happen with or without physical side effects.

Many people who have stress and develop panic attacks have these because of something in the past that they haven't dealt with, stress addiction, or something that they're afraid of that might occur that hasn't happened yet.

A panic attack is a sense of impending doom, even if nothing bad is going on at the moment or they're not in any danger. These attacks are a clear sign for the person who has them that something needs to be treated so that it can end.

When a panic attack disrupts your daily routine and you have difficulty being able to carry on, this a severe episode and may need professional treatment. As a result of your mental health suffering because of stress, you can start feeling dissatisfied with life.

You just feel like something is missing. This can happen when you're not happy with the person you are. You might experience self-doubt along with this dissatisfaction. You might also have low self-esteem and you don't like what you see when you look in the mirror.

You don't like your job, your relationships, or where you stand in life. It's at this point that many people start turning to coping addictions to try to fill the void and feel better about themselves and their lives.

Discovering Where Your Stress Stems From

Stress doesn't just spring up for no reason. There's always something that drives it and it can come from more than one direction at the same time. But if you know where it comes from, then it can help you know how to deal with it.

Work is a big cause of stress. You might get overworked because you're working too many hours. This happens to a lot of people when they work long days, long schedules without a day off or overtime.

But it can also happen when you work on projects or tasks that require a lot of mental focus. You might have work stress because of the relationship you have with your coworkers or your boss.

It might be that there's no cohesiveness and no one really works as a team. There might be infighting, bickering and blaming going on. But it could also be that at your job you just don't feel fulfilled.

You're not happy there and this can cause you stress. Lack of time is another cause of stress. This happens when it feels like you're so on the go - whether physically, mentally or both – that you can barely catch your breath.

Your schedule is packed from morning to night. You don't have time to eat right or exercise and you're always having to juggle things. You can't get everything done, so you have to put it off and then you end up feeling guilty.

Money, or rather the lack of it, is a huge area of life that can cause stress. This kind of stress usually occurs when there's not enough money to cover even the minimum that you need to live.

You might struggle to be able to pay your electric bill or other utilities. There might be times when you have to choose between paying a bill or buying groceries. This kind of stress can cause a lot of mental and physical damage because it affects your instinctual survival mechanism.

It's easier to feel more fear or anxiety when you don't have enough money to take care of your basic needs. Maybe you don't have enough money for the things that you want to do.

You can't go on vacation because the funds just aren't there. Or you can't spruce up your home. Sometimes this lack of money can make it difficult to do fun things in life so you don't really get to have a way to de-stress.

You might even feel like all you do is work, go home, sleep and wait for the cycle to begin again the next day. Relationships could be what's causing your stress - especially if you're in a toxic one.

If you're in an intimate relationship and there's a lot of resentment and criticism, that can be a sign that it's toxic. Or maybe you can't trust the other person. There might be little or no communication.

You can have a toxic relationship with your parents that might be the source of your stress. Some signs that this is what's going on could be that your parents are constantly criticizing you or your decisions in life.

They may be demanding and want money or excessive attention. They'll send you on a guilt trip if you tell them no about anything. If you make them angry, they might give you the silent treatment.

Your friends can be a source of stress, too. Your friendship is filled with drama. They don't listen to your boundaries and take more than they give. They might put you down and act like they were just joking with their unkind statements or behaviors.

Children can also be a cause of stress. They can be disrespectful, uncaring of your opinion, unwilling to listen or to change behaviors that are emotionally damaging to you. If they're adults and have children of their own, they might use their children as a control method.

They might start by saying something like, "You don't get to see the kids unless you do…" whatever it is they want. Or they'll freeze you out of their lives if they don't like something you say.

You might feel like you're walking on eggshells. Anytime you feel like that, it's a sign of stress as well as a sign of a toxic relationship and something needing to change. Parenting can be a huge source of stress.

You might have kids who are out of control. They might be disrespectful and manipulative. They might shout and argue, call you names, fight with their siblings and never follow the rules.

Or it could be that you're all alone in parenting. This can happen to single parents, but it can also happen to parents in a relationship when one is the only person taking care of the kids.

It can be stressful to feel like you have no help dealing with the kids. Health woes can be a cause of stress. If you're always in pain, this can cause you to become anxious or depressed.

You might worry about how you're going to be able to function. Maybe you have headaches that steal a lot of your energy as well as cause you frustration. Or maybe your health is bad because you have something more serious, such as diabetes or cancer.

Living with a disease, especially if it's a scary one, causes you stress because the mental effort it takes to deal with the care and worries about the future. Superficial stress is the kind of stress that happens over small things.

This might be something like the paperboy throws your newspaper too far or hits your door with it. It could be that someone in your house has an annoying habit like not putting the cap back on the toothpaste or leaving wet towels on the floor.

Even though these seem insignificant, they can still stress you. But if you track what's behind your stress, you can find relief. Write down what caused your stress and what was going on with your emotions during the moment of stress.

Once you know where it comes from and what triggers it, then you'll have the knowledge that you need to create a plan to attack the stress and get rid of it or manage it whenever it occurs.

Flipping the Stress Switch to the Off Position

It is important that you look at the stress causes and find a way to greatly reduce them or totally eliminate then from your daily activities.

There are things you can do, beginning right now.

If work is a huge stress factor – start looking at other options. You need the income, but you can begin looking at how to find a better job.

Create a new resume. Look into online education. Would you rather be in another department? What is needed to be considered for a job transfer?

We all only have 24 hours in the day. Finding a way to manage everything we need to do plus have some breathing room for ourselves is important.

Make a list (or use a planner) and write down every single thing you do in a week. It may leave you speechless.

Look at each thing you did. Did you go to the grocery store four times? That may be an easy one to change.

Do you delegate tasks at home and at work (if possible)?

Do your children have a chore chart?

You're one person. You can't work, run errands, take care of home responsibilities, be there for a significant other, raise kids, spend time with your family and manage finances alone.

You'll break before you ever run out of items on your to do list. When there are more responsibilities than there are time and energy, get others to share the load. Someone else can pitch in with the home responsibilities, and with the kids.

Divide up whatever needs to be done and get the entire family involved. When you want relief from stress, you need to break any habit that might be fueling that stress.

If you currently have some money issues – guess what? We all have had them at one time or another. You can and will get through them. Sometimes the most stressful part is just confronting the debt. Are you paying the minimum payment which basically almost all goes to the interest?

I'm not going to tell you to not eat out or to cut out your favorite fall latte. I am going to suggest taking a look at expenses.

If your bank has a "round up" program – sign up. A Round Up program (it may be called something different where you live) is a program that funnels your spare "change" to a separate account. So if you use your debit card for gas and spend $29.01, the remaining 99 cents goes into a separate account. Don't knock it, I accrued over four hundred dollars last year without even thinking about it and I don't use my debit card a lot either.

Taking control of your finances is empowering and squashes a stress factor.

Learning how to say no and not overextend yourself be it money or time is also a way to reduce stress.

Reducing stress may mean really looking at some relationships in your life. You will know which one(s). Are there some people who are like a weight around your neck? Sometimes you can't cut ties with someone due to work or family but recognizing they are a source of stress gives you the opportunity to confront this is an area in your life you will need to adjust.

Raising a family may be one of the most stressful things you will ever do. Taking care of an elderly family member also ranks near the top. You love them of course and wouldn't trade them for the world but sometimes the stress builds so fast.

Reset yourself to let go of some of the things that cause you stress. If you take care of an elderly person, put their medications on an auto refill. Look into meal delivery or meal planning. Crockpots can be your best friend. Find recipes that are easy, filling and delicious. Buy the crockpot liners – the couple dollars they cost are worth the time they save you later.

It is simple things like the ones mentioned above that can and will free up time for you.

If your health or weight or not having time to exercise add stress, look at what you can do to improve that area. Even simple steps, like parking in the back of a parking lot and walking, give you at least a place to begin. No matter how small it may seem, you are taking action and that is what counts.

Look really hard at what is causing your stress. When something is insignificant, don't trade your mental well-being or your physical well-being by putting up with it. When something bothers you, decide once and for all that you're done with it. Then let it go and don't look back.

Curb Your Public Complaining

This often a hard habit to break. Yet sometimes it seems to be what helps so much – being able to complain to someone else.

Everyone complains on some level. It is when it becomes all consuming. I think we have all known at least one person we have ducked away from or tried to avoid as they were a chronic whiner and complainer. You don't want to be labeled as that person.

Public complaining may also create secondhand stress. The person you are complaining to may become stressed also.

Take a look at things you say and also things you post on social media.

Take a second and consider the effect it might be having on those you care about and then decide if it's really worth griping about openly. Sometimes, people who practice public complaining aren't aware that they're doing it as often as they are.

This is why you need to check yourself to see if this is your issue. Take a look at your social media feeds. Look at what you've posted and at what you've responded to. Reread your comments in any groups or forums. What percentage is negative?

This doesn't mean that your stress isn't legitimate.

It only means that you're better off learning how to stop complaining. When you vent on social media, it doesn't help to lessen your stress. Whatever is bothering you didn't go away just because you posted about it and now others may start to think that your life is one big drama.

If you want to change your habit of public complaining, learn to look for the good that happened in the day. There will always be something - even if it's a small thing. Practice being grateful for the little things.

Replace Bad Stress Habits with Good Ones

When you are stressed, it is easy to develop bad habits to help yourself cope with the stress. You may not even notice you are doing so. For example, you may find comfort in eating or online shopping. You may feel like flopping on the sofa under a blanket instead of taking your afternoon walk.

When you find yourself becoming stressed, it is important to ensure no bad habits are also beginning to be formed. Letting bad habits continue to pile up can lead to health problems.

If you see you already have some bad habits in place, today is the day you will begin changing those bad habits into good habits.

Consistent negative thoughts can lead to health problems. With this habit, you have a tendency to always see the bad in situations. You also project the worst in things that haven't even happened yet.

You don't expect anything good when negative thoughts are your reaction to stress. Bad thoughts are one of the first stress management habits you should work on changing because if you can do that, your emotions will follow.

Replacing bad thoughts with good ones is done through the power of positive thinking. Don't mistake positive thinking for pretending everything is fine. It's not a fake way of going through life.

It only means that there is negative stuff going on, but your view on this is different. Rather than taking a worst case scenario approach, you decide to think about the good that could occur rather than the bad.

To get started using the power of positive thinking, you have to watch how you speak to yourself. This means that you don't let your thoughts have free rein in your mind. Thoughts will pop in and out of your mind.

Positive thinking means that you stay on guard against any thoughts that are negative in nature. It means that you become more aware when any optimism has given way to pessimism.

You stop negative thoughts and figure out what the truth is because many negative thoughts aren't based on truth. Instead, they're rooted in misinformation or unhealed emotional wounds.

So you have to question whether or not these thoughts are valid. When you practice the habit of positive thinking, not only does it improve your stress and mental well-being, but it benefits your physical health, too.

You can boost your immune system and lower your blood pressure. You'll have lower levels of anxiety and depression - plus, you'll be better equipped to cope when stressful things do happen.

If you look at a situation and only notice all the bad stuff, that's a sign that you need to work on this. Or if you get fifty good comments on a project at work, but one person said something disparaging, so you don't remember the 49 good comments - only the one that was negative, it means you need to refocus on what's important.

If your thoughts lean toward shaming or blaming yourself even when you don't know all of the facts, that's a symptom of negative thinking. This usually happens when you're projecting what someone else is thinking or doing and you decide that some how it's your fault.

Perfectionism is another sign of negative thinking. You believe that if you don't get something 100% right, everything you're trying is wrong. One way to address negativity like this is by practicing deep breathing when you're in turmoil rather than shallow breathing.

Your body has two systems that run your body. One is called the parasympathetic nervous system and the other one is your sympathetic nervous system. When you get stressed, your sympathetic nervous system kicks into high gear and speeds up your heart rate, jacks up your blood pressure and prepares you to run or fight.

But when you take deep breaths, your stress gets soothed because it taps into your parasympathetic system, which is responsible for releasing stress, lowering your heartbeat and helping you to calm down.

So when you're in turmoil, turn to deep breathing and you'll stop that stress response in its tracks. Stress can make you want to go off alone and dwell on the problem. You work it over and over in your mind until your thoughts are in a frenzy.

That's a bad habit that needs to be eliminated. You can do this by turning to laughter and comedy. You might have heard the saying that laughter is the best medicine. It's true.

Laughing offers many benefits and by replacing a bad stress habit with this good one, you can find inner peace. Learn how to find things to laugh about even in the midst of chaos.

Deliberately seek out stuff that's funny. This might be a funny story, a show, a movie, a book, quotes, or spending time with people who make you laugh or smile. Laugh about the mistakes that you make.

See the humor whenever something goes wrong. When you develop this habit, it boosts your mental well-being as well as improves your physical health, too. By laughing, your brain gives you a dose of the feel-good chemicals named endorphins, and this natural high immediately eases stress because it calms the response system.

You'll end up with lower blood pressure, fewer aches and pains and a calmer digestive system because laughter relaxes the entire body. You'll also strengthen your immune system.

A Breathing Technique That Works to Shut Down Stress

I hold expert certification in NLP (Neuro-linguistic Programming). One of the very first exercises I learned during my certification process was a breathing technique to reduce and eliminate stress. This isn't just any technique. It is one used by Navy SEALS. And it works.

Stress and anxiety trigger neurocircuitry that was designed to be used sparingly to deal with life-or-death threats, not on a daily basis, as a response to siting in a bottleneck of a traffic jam, a toxic boss or overbearing work overload.

Research indicates that there is a correlation between the way you breathe and the way you think and feel.

When you are stressed, your body naturally goes into the "fight or flight" mode. In other words, your body perceives a threat – in this case whatever is causing the stress. When we are stressed, our breathing pattern also changes.

Learning a breathing exercise, the same one used by Navy SEALS, provides the ideal balance a body needs to calm down. Breathing in this manner provides the right mix of oxygen and carbon dioxide in your blood, thus setting off mechanisms inside your body that move the body towards relaxation and away from stress.

And what better techniques to master than the ones practiced by one of America's finest Special Ops forces?

To stay focused and calm, SEALs practice these two simple controlled breathing techniques that help them take the stress off amazingly fast. I will add, speaking from experience, I was amazed how easy and fast this exercise was and is one I use as needed for the past few years.

The difference between tactical breathing and box breathing is that box breathing includes a breath hold after the inhale and exhale.

Navy SEALS Box Breathing technique

Box Breathing

Four incredibly easy simple steps –

Close your eyes. Breathe in through your nose while counting to four slowly.

Hold your breath inside while counting slowly to four. Try not to clamp your mouth or nose shut.

Begin to slowly exhale for 4 seconds.

Repeat steps 1 to 3 at least four times

The idea behind it is that it helps you take control of your automatic breathing patterns to train your breath for optimal health and performance

In your head, picture a box with equal sides.

Inhale, the holding of the breath, and exhale are all four counts (four seconds approx.). "As you take in a breath, for four counts, visualize traveling up one side of the square.

Then, you imagine moving across the top of the square during the four counts of holding your breath.

Then follow the breath down the right side of the box on the exhale and watch it travel across the bottom of the square on the breath hold, following the exhale.

Repeat the pattern.

The visualization of the box provides a focus for your attention thus allowing you to get into the flow of rhythmic breathing.

When we do this box breathing exercise we are doing so through our nostrils. This helps us pull the air deep into our lungs.

The effect of this exercise is noticeable very quickly. I am still amazed over how easy it was and how fast it worked. I should also add – I am a mouth breather and was able to convert easily to breathing through my nose.

Does Stress Give You Permission to Indulge?

Many bad habits are covered under the word stress. Stress can affect you, but it shouldn't be something that you use to negatively impact your life. What happens when you deal with stress is that you'll form either good or bad habits.

Some people like experiencing stress because then it gives them an excuse for whatever they're doing that's not that good for them. They might say to themselves that they had a hard day or they're just overloaded with too much on their plates so they're going to need to have a glass (or several) of wine. Or they may decide they need to do some shopping to "unwind" and online shopping makes this even easier.

What you don't realize is that this can become a habit because it's created a reward pathway in the brain. You'll develop a link between stress and wanting to do something you enjoy but that can hurt you in the end.

This is also the way that a stress addiction develops. You'll start to crave the stress because you know what will be waiting for you as a way of soothing that stress. Some people use smoking as their stress excuse.

Office workers who complain about the stress they deal with on the job usually say they need a smoke break. They do this because they want to smoke, and stress is their permission slip.

When you're feeling that frustration or anxiety because of work and you just want to get to that cigarette, it's become a crutch that you use. You probably already know that smoking isn't good for your health but using it as an excuse makes you feel better about this bad habit.

You might have created this permission for yourself because you just had more work piled on you or your hours changed, and everything is more mentally demanding at work. Maybe your boss expects more from you.

Smoking actually induces more stress and heightens the reaction as well as the effects of stress. When you smoke, it raises your blood pressure just like stress does. Your heart rate will speed up because of the cigarette.

Those who use smoking as permission to indulge themselves due to stress experience a temporary break and feel good only because nicotine reacts in your body to help stimulate the release of feel-good chemicals.

So for a little while, you might feel wonderful. But that feeling will go away and you'll end up feeling more stressed than ever as well as having damaged your health. Overeating is another area where you might be giving yourself permission to indulge.

You'll find that there are a lot of jokes about eating and stress like eating a pint of ice cream whenever you're stressed. Though it's meant as a joke, there's a lot of truth behind that.

Over-indulging in food is a common way that people use the stress excuse. They want to eat the things that aren't good for them and may even crave those foods. There may or may not be an emotional connection, too.

This is a reaction that develops as a result of pushing aside the emotions that stress can cause. These stresses can be because of feelings like anxiety or depression, but they can also be because you feel overwhelmed by responsibilities, or you're dealing with financial or relationship pressure.

When people use overeating as permission to indulge, the food of choice is usually whatever is high in fat, salt or sugar. They'll eat the food, feel better temporarily and think that this indulgence is helping them cope with stress, but it's not.

You can end up gaining weight and feeling worse about yourself as your health worsens. Dangerous behaviors is an indulgence that some people use when they're stressed.

These dangerous behaviors all fall into the categories of things that risk their lives. When people turn to dangerous behaviors, they get an adrenaline high that makes the stress go away.

But as soon as that adrenaline is gone, the stress returns. Some people will turn to drugs and think that the stress they're going through gives them permission to do this. They believe they're only trying to find an outlet.

Because the drugs eliminate the stress temporarily, they think they've found the right answer. Using drugs causes the body's nervous system to react. While it might feel like taking drugs eases stress, the act actually increases the stress your body encounters.

Plus, because it works on the brain's reward system, taking drugs easily causes an addiction. The more stress you encounter, the greater the craving for drugs will be.

Even sex can be used as permission to indulge due to stress. Some people use this as an excuse to indulge because it does relieve stress. Thanks to the boost of endorphins you get, it relaxes both the mind and the body. But sex used to deal with anxiety or the frustration stemming from sex can also become an addiction.

Interrupting Your Usual Stress Reactions

Everyone reacts to stress in their own way. But some of the ways that you might be responding to stress can actually make it worse. Or it can lead you to make choices that are harmful both in the short and long term.

By learning better ways to react to stress, you'll be able to break the stress cycle and find peace immediately without having to wait. Emotional Freedom Technique or EFT is one of the solutions that you can use to find stress relief.

When you get stressed, it can hit out of the blue and you won't get to pick the location where you're at when this happens. For stress that comes on suddenly and catches you unaware, you want a quick fix that's reliable, yet doesn't announce to everyone around you that you're dealing with something.

You can use this technique at home, at the office, or even when you're in public because it's a discreet method to use to restore calm. When to use EFT is a matter of personal choice, but most people use it the moment that their stress is triggered because by doing so, they regain control of their emotions.

This enables them to respond calmly to upsetting situations. It can be used when something like anxiety or irritability is present. It can also be used to help you not react in anger or with sadness.

Plus, it can help to restore order to your thoughts so that you don't react by saying or doing something that you might later regret. When you perform the movements taught in EFT, it might not fix the situation, but it resolves whatever upheaval you're dealing with on the spot.

There's no wrong time to use EFT to get relief. You don't even have to wait until you're in the middle of a stressful situation and you also don't have to wait until the stress actually hits you.

It can also be used as a preventative measure. If you know that you're going have to face a stressful situation or person, you can use EFT to help calm you down so that you don't let the stress build before you encounter the trigger.

The practice of using EFT allows you to face the situation rather than turning to ways that aren't working or that cover up stress. By tapping on the right points of your body using the technique, you tap into the energy.

It's encountering this energy that allows you to be able to direct how you respond to stress. Visualization or guided imagery can also be used to bring you out of a stressful situation.

These resources can give you fast relief from stress by allowing you to picture a more peaceful place in your mind's eye. This is when your focus turns internal rather than remains on what's going on outwardly.

You focus on what's calm and it allows you to distance yourself immediately from the stress. The visualization that you use can be what you consider your happy place. Some people visualize a sunny beach and imagine the warmth of the sand beneath their feet.

They hear the water as it rolls in. They feel the stickiness from the salty water as the wind blows across the ocean. Or they might visualize being in a flower covered meadow and looking up at a bright blue summer sky. They see the white clouds lazily floating past.

Because they make you feel relaxed, whatever the images are that you choose to use, they help to calm the emotions, slow the shallow, rapid breaths and lower the blood pressure.

As you visualize, the effects of the stress drain from your body and you're able to achieve control immediately. As you interrupt your stress reactions with visualization, you would use deeper breathing to help calm the reaction your body gets from your nervous system.

Guided imagery works similar to visualization, except there's someone guiding you through what you visualize. Both of these resources can work in just seconds. You can regain control of your stress reaction by mentally picturing your relaxation space and by tuning in to how that space affects your senses.

You would tune in to what you feel and see as well as what you hear. When you need quick peace to alleviate stress, you can also use self-hypnosis or meditation. With self-hypnosis, it just means that you're redirecting your thoughts and actions so that you're not focusing on the emotions or the stressor.

Using this therapeutic approach causes you to relax and allows your body to quickly release stress tension. You can use this technique to stop the anxiety that the stress is causing you to feel and when you're faced with a situation that creates stress, you can use this type of hypnosis to overcome any automated reactions.

Plus, it works to break any cycle of bad stress habits. When you use self-hypnosis, it works similar to meditation by tapping into the subconscious in order to effect a change. To learn how to use this effectively, there are plenty of resources you can use to train yourself.

Meditation, like self-hypnosis, works to relax you in the moment when you're faced with a stressor. However, they're not the same thing. With hypnosis, you enter a different level of focus.

When stress is affecting you and your emotions are heightened, meditation can restore calm and it doesn't take a long time. You can accomplish peace with meditation even with just seconds of use.

It works on the mind-body connection. When you practice meditation, you're looking inward to halt the racing thoughts that are creating or acerbating the stress. By interrupting this pattern, you break the link between the stress and whatever negative emotion you're experiencing.

With meditation, you can inhale through your nose, hold the breath for a short count, then exhale. Doing this pushes out the stress and restores calm. Pick whatever method works best for you or use them in a rotation to alleviate your stress.

Learning to Live a Stress-Free Life

The reason people choose to engage in dangerous actions when they're stressed is because it gives them a dopamine release. This lets them feel good. While they might get a temporary break from the stress, you want to learn how to live a stress-free life rather than constantly seeking an unsafe way to handle your stress.

Find activities or things that you implement that are safe, but which still give you that emotional high you get from heightened emotions. This not only feeds your need for the natural high, but it can help you learn to handle stress in ways that are positive and good for you.

That might mean pushing yourself outside of your comfort zone. These new ways that you use to get an emotional high could be either physical or emotional. For example, it could be that you turn to something like learning how to do rock climbing or climbing a mountain.

Or maybe you decide that you want to go skiing for the first time. It might be that you push yourself to take part in regular activities that are made to pump up your adrenaline. This could be something like vigorous exercise.

Or it might be fast-paced dancing. Some people turn to sports and join an amateur league. When you push yourself in ways that are new and make you feel a little unsure, it can raise your emotions and give you that same heightened state that stress once gave you.

A new way could be doing something like beating a clock. You challenge yourself to get something done under a deadline or under budget at work. Whatever you choose to challenge yourself with makes you feel good and excited about the effort.

It could be a relational challenge that you use to feel that emotional high. This might mean something like reaching out to a new member of your community or joining an organization that engages in activities that benefit an area.

Learning to live a stress-free life might mean choosing to find activities in your down time that you can do. These activities could be positive things like hobbies or projects, and they can be in different areas of your life.

Whatever activities that you choose should better your life or give you more quality time with your family or friends. At work, you could learn a new skill such as programming that helps you get your stuff done more efficiently.

Or you could discover how to master a new technology. The challenge of learning something new also increases the level of dopamine in your body, which makes you get that same high you get from stress, but in a better way.

You can attend a networking event or try out for a new position at work. Doing this could increase your value to the company and help alleviate work-related stress because you're doing something positive as well as being proactive.

At home, you could let go of things that demand your time, but which aren't all that important and this can free up time for you to do things that help you live stress-free.

You can organize your home.

By getting rid of chaos, you invite in tranquility. You can also engage in activities like painting, drawing, or doing fun home projects that you've always wanted to do. With your family and friends, you can take a class that interests you such as photography.

Or you can join an exercise club with a group of friends and work out together. You can spend time with your kids going to a theme park or spend time learning a fun activity like biking or going on a picnic or redecorating their bedroom.

You could take the entire family along and go outdoors for geocaching. Not only are these exciting things to do, but you'll all benefit from the time you get to spend with each other.

Stress is going to happen because that's just the way life goes. But that doesn't mean that you have to give in to it and it doesn't mean that you have to let it linger. There are coping mechanisms that you can learn so that you're okay when stress arises.

Understand that stress is something that you have to handle, but it's not something that's permanent. When stress happens to you, the first thing you need to do is be wary of how you talk to yourself.

Self-talk that feeds the stress always makes everything seem worse. Plus, it heightens your emotions and can convince you of things that aren't true, such as a thought that nothing is ever going to get any better.

If you tell yourself that what you're going through is the worst thing ever, then you'll start acting like it is and head for a downward spiral deep into the symptoms of stress. Pay attention to what you say.

Try to speak only positive things because what you hear can cause you to believe or behave a certain way. Be calm and don't overreact. This is the step that usually trips up a lot of people.

They don't pause to think things through. A stress event occurs and they immediately react to that stress. Usually when stress occurs, if you've had a problem dealing with it in the past, it can be really easy to feel that tug to just turn to whatever you thought worked for you back then.

You might reach for alcohol or turn to food as a way of trying to calm yourself. But to live a stress-free life, you have to make up your mind that you're not going to make self-destructive choices in the moments when stress hits.

Choosing something that's self-destructive might make you feel better temporarily, but in the end, this decision will only make things worse. Remind yourself that what's going on isn't going to last forever, that you will get through it and be okay.

Keep an Eye Out for Old Habits

You're driving down the road and all of a sudden, a warning light comes on in your car's dash. You ignore the light and keep right on driving until your vehicle quits and can't move another mile.

You wouldn't ignore a warning light on your car's dash if you knew it was going to lead to trouble, yet many people ignore the warning signs that they're struggling with stress and emotional upheaval.

Checking in on your emotional health and stress levels is like looking at your car's dash. The sooner that you spot trouble, the quicker you can intervene and prevent a small problem from becoming a major one.

Evaluate your stress levels daily. Ask yourself how you're feeling but don't just settle for that. When you ask yourself how you're feeling, go beyond that to uncover why you're feeling the way that you are.

If you're angry, prod yourself until you uncover why you're angry. If you're sad or feeling anxious, keep looking within until you locate the answer. When you know the answer, you can understand what you must do in order to get better.

It could be that you're feeling down because you just didn't sleep well the night before. Or it could be that you're struggling with feelings of being overwhelmed because a project at work just isn't going right.

Look for patterns in your life that can hint that stress is on the rise. Maybe you notice that you always feel sad after you've spent time with a certain friend. Or you have a co-worker that never fails to push your buttons.

You should schedule a check in with yourself regularly until you pinpoint the sources of your stress. For some people, this might need to be once a day. For others, it could be every week or every month.

When you realize that you've begun to fall back into the same old habits, distance yourself from that stressor if you can. If you can't, do something positive to replace the emotional upset from the stressor.

For example, if you noticed that you get stressed after spending time with family and you've started emotional eating again, then plan a relaxing lunch meeting or shopping date with a good friend.

What can also be helpful is to ask friends or family to tell you when you seem stressed out. Ask them to alert you if they see any changes in your behavior. This can be helpful because sometimes you can't see your own issues starting to crop up.

You might not be aware that you're experiencing changes in your mental or emotional health because maybe you've just been too busy or the signs have been too subtle for you to notice.

But family and friends can be helpful because they can be an early alert system letting you know when something is off with you. Make sure that you ask for clarification. If a friend or family member says that you seem down, ask them what they mean – but don't get defensive.

Because this could be anything from them noticing that you have low energy to them seeing that you're avoiding activities that you once loved. They might recognize that your sleeping or eating patterns have changed.

By asking them for clarification, it can help you determine what your next step should be and also help you start to recognize the problem yourself later on. Be willing to listen to what they point out.

Sometimes it can be tempting to become defensive, especially if you fall back into an old habit that you enjoyed, like drinking too much. If you get defensive, it shuts down the conversation and keeps you from hearing information that might be helpful.

Ask your family and friends for suggestions. If someone is alerting you to a problem, ask them to help you come up with a solution if you're not sure what to do next. For example, if you seem to have low energy, your family member might have noticed that you're skipping out on sleep or that you're not eating right.

You can keep an eye out for old habits by maintaining a journal. Having a journal can help you decompress each day so that you keep tabs on rising issues. This helps you to get the stress out, but it also allows you to step back from whatever issue is going on.

Sometimes getting the emotion out lets you think more clearly. It can also help you to come up with the right solution as well to be more objective about the stress you're dealing with.

Review your journal each week or month. Do this to look for patterns that might signal deeper issues. You don't want to deal with stress just on the surface. You want to make sure that you get down to the roots so that you can remove it from your life.

It could be that you turn to binge eating after having an upsetting conversation with a friend, family member or work colleague. That means that there are issues there that need to be resolved or you need to find a better coping skill so that you don't let that old habit get reestablished in your life.

Be honest in your journal. Even if what you're thinking or feeling is dark and ugly, get it out. It's human to experience emotions and some of those feelings can be quite raw and difficult.

But by being honest, you get to the heart of what's really going on. Make sure that you recognize your limits. If you're struggling with your old habits, know when you should reach out for additional help or other resources.

When you can't handle the stress on your own and the bad habit seems to be the only solution you come up with, talk to someone else, learn a new coping strategy or add more to the solutions that you're already using.

Workbook

You've reached the workbook section of this book. All answers are yours – no one else will have the same answers as you will.

It is really important to be honest with yourself as you go through each question.

Self-Assessment

To begin the workbook section of this book, you'll be doing a quick self-assessment, so you have a gauge on the level of your anger and resentment levels.

Remember, this is your book and your life. These are your confidential answers and no one else's.

You'll be using a scale of 1 to 5 to rate your answers. You can tally your score at the end and see the results.

1 - Never

2 - Rarely

3 - Occasionally

4 – Frequently

5.- Most of the time

1. When someone criticizes me, it makes me angry inside.

2. If I'm being ignored, it upsets me and makes me feel angry.

3. If I'm being critiqued (such as a job performance review or a new recipe that I made) and the critique is not favorable, it hurts my feelings and I may reply back in an angry manner.

4. When someone tries to change the way I am doing something (such as at work or a task at home), it upsets me as I have my own way of doing things.

5. I become frustrated when I can't solve a problem or figure out a set of instructions.

6. If I'm in an argument, I really need to have "the last word".

7. When people disagree with me, it makes me upset and sometimes angry.

8. If I get in an argument, I often will leave or become verbally aggressive.

9. If I get an argument, I have a hard time backing down, especially if the person is right in my face.

10. I tend to raise my voice to be in control during a conversation or argument.

11. If someone confronts me in an angry manner, I tend to respond in anger a level above theirs.

12. I'll let small things build up and one day I just blow up over the past situations.

My total score is -

Self-Assessment Score Key Results

If your score falls between 50-60

You are quick to anger and struggle to cope with the resentment and negative feelings that come with it. You need to learn positive ways to deal with it, to verbalize it appropriately, and do so without escalating situations.

If your score falls between 40-49

You react when something really gets your goat. You just need to make time to learn what triggers your anger and resentment to figure out how best to manage it appropriately. Learning to be assertive without being aggressive is a key skill for someone who often falls into resentment.

If your score falls between 20-39

You are slow to anger, but you may still struggle with resentment. When you feel yourself holding things in, assertiveness skills would help you express yourself appropriately.

If your score falls between 0 and 18.

You're a laid-back individual and you find it easy to stay calm under pressure. That doesn't mean you're immune to resentment, but you tend to cope better with your feelings than others.

Exercise 1 Overcoming Resentment

Anger often leads to resentment so it's important to know how prone to anger you are. Getting to grips with your anger triggers can help you avoid resentment in the future. Now, let's focus on managing the resentment you are dealing with *now*.

Before you can overcome resentment, you need to idea the source of it. Answer the questions below to get a better idea of what you are dealing with and the source.

What event(s) or person(s) is creating your resentment issue?

_____

_____

_____

_____

_____

_____

_____

_____

_____

_____

_____

_____

_____

_____

_____

_____

What did each of these events or people do that led you to hold this level of resentment?

_____

_____

_____

_____

_____

_____

_____

_____

_____

_____

_____

_____

_____

_____

_____

_____

_____

_____

_____

_____

_____

_____

_____

_____

_____

When you look back on these offenses now, are they real? Or are they imagined or perhaps a bit exaggerated?

_____

_____

_____

_____

_____

_____

_____

_____

_____

_____

_____

_____

_____

_____

_____

_____

_____

_____

_____

_____

_____

_____

_____

_____

What emotions do you experience when you are faced with this person or event?

_____

_____

_____

_____

_____

_____

_____

_____

_____

_____

_____

_____

_____

_____

_____

_____

_____

_____

_____

_____

_____

_____

_____

What emotions do you experience when you think about this person or event?

_____

_____

_____

_____

_____

_____

_____

_____

_____

_____

_____

_____

_____

_____

_____

_____

_____

_____

_____

_____

_____

_____

_____

_____

How do those emotions impact your life?

In terms of your attitude and mindset towards yourself and your future, how have these resentments influenced you?

_____

_____

_____

_____

_____

_____

_____

_____

_____

_____

_____

_____

_____

_____

_____

_____

_____

_____

_____

_____

_____

_____

_____

How stifled has your personal growth and development been as a result of the resentment you carry?

_____

_____

_____

_____

_____

_____

_____

_____

_____

_____

_____

_____

_____

_____

_____

_____

_____

_____

_____

_____

_____

_____

_____

Now that you have identified the people and events for which you hold resentment, it's time to reframe how you view the past, as well as your present and future.

Due to your resentment, what biased thinking are you trapped in?

_____

_____

_____

_____

_____

_____

_____

_____

_____

_____

_____

_____

_____

_____

_____

_____

_____

_____

_____

_____

_____

When you purge yourself of this resentment, how will that help you develop a positive mindset?

_____

_____

_____

_____

_____

_____

_____

_____

_____

_____

_____

_____

_____

_____

_____

_____

_____

_____

_____

_____

_____

_____

_____

_____

How can you open yourself to the idea of working through your resentment?

What holds you back from appropriately expressing your anger?

_____

_____

_____

_____

_____

_____

_____

_____

_____

_____

_____

_____

_____

_____

_____

_____

_____

_____

_____

_____

_____

_____

_____

How hard have you worked to overcome these obstacles?

_____
_____
_____
_____
_____
_____
_____
_____
_____
_____
_____
_____
_____
_____
_____
_____
_____
_____
_____
_____
_____
_____
_____
_____
_____

What new behavior(s) could you develop to express your feelings appropriately to work past resentment?

_____

_____

_____

_____

_____

_____

_____

_____

_____

_____

_____

_____

_____

_____

_____

_____

_____

_____

_____

_____

_____

_____

_____

_____

Imagine yourself free of your resentment, how will that positively impact your life?

_____

_____

_____

_____

_____

_____

_____

_____

_____

_____

_____

_____

_____

_____

_____

_____

_____

_____

_____

_____

_____

_____

_____

_____

Think about and list behavior(s) can you adopt or strengthen to ensure you don't take on any new resentments.

_____

_____

_____

_____

_____

_____

_____

_____

_____

_____

_____

_____

_____

_____

_____

_____

_____

_____

_____

_____

_____

_____

_____

_____

_____

Exercise 2 - Empathy Towards Others

Now that you have thought about how to change your beliefs and attitude, you can address the largest issue and release the resentment.

For each person that you have flagged as having resentment over, you'll be writing a letter. You do not need to send each letter so don't hold back on saying whatever you want to say.

This workbook section has a page for you to do so. You can use the page for one letter or use your own paper – whichever you feel most comfortable doing.

In this letter you will list out all of the offenses that have transpired with this person that have caused resentment.

Explain why you felt the way you did, why you didn't like their treatment of you and how it made you feel at the time and how it still makes you feel.

When you are finished, take a few minutes to read what you have written. This is the past. Let it go and move on. You can do something symbolic such as burning each letter (safely of course), hand shredding each one, cutting up with scissors or, a favorite one – using a shredder.

While you are shredding, cutting it up or burning it, imagine all your resentments going with the letter. Let your resentments go. If you feel able to forgive them, do so while doing this exercise. If you don't feel like forgiving them, forgive yourself for letting this resentment build up as it did.

It is in your past now. Done. Gone. The slate is clean.

My Letter

Empathy Towards Others

Empathy is the ability to sense other people's emotions, coupled with the ability to imagine what someone else might be thinking or feeling.

Often we focus on our own stress and resentment and forget (not intentionally) how others may be feeling or reacting.

For this exercise we are going to put the shoe on the other foot and take a look using empathy.

_____
_____
_____
_____
_____
_____
_____
_____
_____
_____
_____
_____
_____
_____
_____
_____
_____
_____
_____
_____
_____

Consider the resentments you wrote about above. Have you ever done anything similar to someone you know? Write an example of when you have hurt, offended, or disappointed another whether by word or deed even if it wasn't intentional.

_____

_____

_____

_____

_____

_____

_____

_____

_____

_____

_____

_____

_____

_____

_____

_____

_____

_____

_____

_____

_____

_____

_____

_____

How do you think that impacted your relationships with this person?

_____

_____

_____

_____

_____

_____

_____

_____

_____

_____

_____

_____

_____

_____

_____

_____

_____

_____

_____

_____

_____

_____

_____

What emotions do you think they would have experienced as a result of this event or situation?

_____

_____

_____

_____

_____

_____

_____

_____

_____

_____

_____

_____

_____

_____

_____

_____

_____

_____

_____

_____

_____

_____

_____

What emotions do you think they experience when they come face to face with you?

_____

_____

_____

_____

_____

_____

_____

_____

_____

_____

_____

_____

_____

_____

_____

_____

_____

_____

_____

_____

_____

_____

_____

_____

Yes, you may have hurt or upset someone. You, like them, are only human. No one is without fault, we all make mistakes, and remembering that you are capable of the same is an important part of the healing process.

Moving forward, think about those situations differently now. Think about how you may have contributed to those situations even if unintentionally.

The best way to heal anger, resentment, and guilt is to take responsibility for our actions and choices. For example, perhaps you resent someone for canceling on something that was important to you. But when you think back now, you realize they were at a difficult time in their life and were just trying to do the best they could.

There are often countless factors in motion regarding why we do the things we do. They churn under the surface of our lives and sometimes build up into arguments, fights and break ups.

_____

_____

_____

_____

_____

_____

_____

_____

_____

_____

_____

_____

_____

_____

_____

_____

_____

_____

Think of someone you may owe an apology to and why.

You're only human. You may choose to address the issues with the people you feel as though you owe an apology to. This is only appropriate if contacting the person will not upset or cause them harm.

They don't owe you forgiveness just like you don't owe forgiveness to someone who has harmed you.

However, if you know it will have a positive result to apologize to them directly, you may want to consider making the effort to do so. If you have judged someone due to their behavior without recognizing your own behavior, you're not alone. We have all done that at some time or another.

In the space below, write a letter of forgiveness (whether it's to yourself or someone else). If there is more than one person you think you owe an apology to then write those letters separately. It's a helpful exercise to process emotions and the better you become at processing your feelings, the better you grow at addressing issues head-on rather than allowing them to simmer under the surface until they boil over. You do not need to deliver these letters or mail them.

_____

_____

_____

_____

_____

_____

_____

_____

_____

_____

_____

_____

_____

_____

_____

_____

_____

_____

_____

_____

_____

_____

Exercise 3 - Handling Stress and Resentment with Gratitude

Developing an attitude of gratitude will help you handle stress and resentment much more easily.

You've taken a very large leap in beginning and now finishing this workbook.

Our final exercise is gratitude prompts.

Validate yourself and all you've accomplished thus far. There is much more ahead of you and you have the tools to handle stress and resentment.

_____

_____

_____

_____

_____

_____

_____

_____

_____

_____

_____

_____

_____

_____

_____

_____

Name 5 things you love about yourself and why.

_____

_____

_____

_____

_____

_____

_____

_____

_____

_____

_____

_____

_____

_____

_____

_____

_____

_____

_____

_____

_____

_____

What's something that you're looking forward to doing?

What's a simple pleasure that you're grateful for?

What's something that you grateful to have today that you didn't have a year ago?

Write about a happy memory.

What's an accomplishment you're proud of?

What possession that makes your life easier and why?

Name something or someone that makes you feel safe and write the reasons why.

_____

_____

_____

_____

_____

_____

_____

_____

_____

_____

_____

_____

_____

_____

_____

_____

_____

_____

_____

_____

_____

_____

_____

How are you able to help others?

Write about a friend that you're grateful for.

_____

_____

_____

_____

_____

_____

_____

_____

_____

_____

_____

_____

_____

_____

_____

_____

_____

_____

_____

_____

_____

_____

_____

Write about a teacher or mentor that you're grateful for.

Write about a family member that you're grateful for.

What did you accomplish today?

What's one of your personality traits that you're grateful for? Why?

_____

_____

_____

_____

_____

_____

_____

_____

_____

_____

_____

_____

_____

_____

_____

_____

_____

_____

_____

_____

_____

_____

_____

_____

_____

What mistake or failure are you grateful for? Why?

What skill(s) do you have that you're grateful for? Why?

_____

_____

_____

_____

_____

_____

_____

_____

_____

_____

_____

_____

_____

_____

_____

_____

_____

_____

_____

_____

_____

_____

_____

_____

_____

_____

Name something that you bought recently that you're grateful for and write why.

_____

_____

_____

_____

_____

_____

_____

_____

_____

_____

_____

_____

_____

_____

_____

_____

_____

_____

_____

_____

_____

_____

What's something that you made recently that you're grateful for? Why?

_____

_____

_____

_____

_____

_____

_____

_____

_____

_____

_____

_____

_____

_____

_____

_____

_____

_____

_____

_____

_____

_____

Look around the room and write about everything you see that you're grateful for.

_____

_____

_____

_____

_____

_____

_____

_____

_____

_____

_____

_____

_____

_____

_____

_____

_____

_____

_____

_____

_____

_____

_____

Write about 3 things you're grateful for today.

Thank You

You've reached the end of this book. I hope that it has provided solutions and a new outlook on handling challenges in your life.

Thank you very much for purchasing and reading this book.

Sincerely,

Diana

www.ingramcontent.com/pod-product-compliance
Lightning Source LLC
Chambersburg PA
CBHW052116020426
42335CB00021B/2789